THE TREEHOUSE JOKE BOOK 2

BY THE INTERNATIONALLY BESTSELLING ANDY GRIFFITHS & TERRY DENTON

MACMILLAN CHILDREN'S BOOKS

First published 2021 in Pan by Pan Macmillan Australia Pty Ltd
1 Market Street, Sydney, New South Wales, Australia, 2000

Published 2021 by Macmillan Children's Books
an imprint of Pan Macmillan
The Smithson, 6 Briset Street, London EC1M 5NR
EU representative: Macmillan Publishers Ireland Limited,
Mallard Lodge, Lansdowne Village, Dublin 4
Associated companies throughout the world
www.panmacmillan.com

ISBN 978-1-5290-4790-5

1 3 5 7 9 8 6 4 2

A CIP catalogue record for this book is available from the British Library.

Typeset in Prater Sans Pro, PMN Caecilia by Seymour Designs
Printed and bound by CPI Group (UK) Ltd, Croydon CR0 4YY

MIX
Paper from
responsible sources
FSC® C116313

CONTENTS

KLUNK!

THUMP!

BARKY & FRIENDS
Hi, I'm Barky the barking dog and the only thing I love more than barking is jokes. Especially jokes about dogs.

My dog has no nose.

How does it smell?

Terrible!

1

Q: In what month do dogs bark the least?

A: February, it's the shortest month!

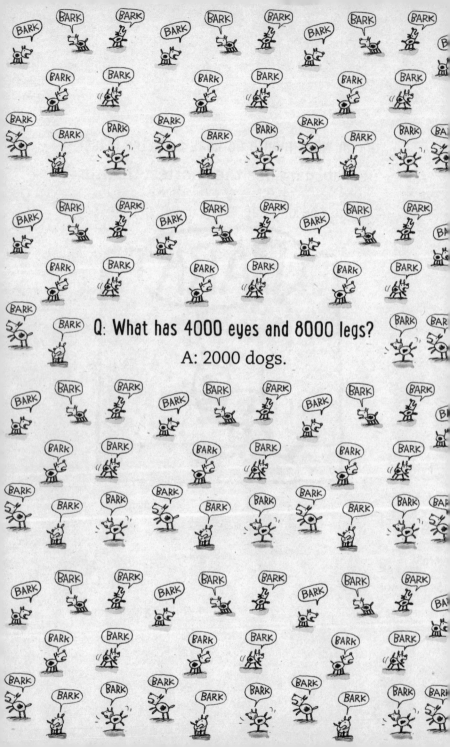

Q: What did the dog say when it sat on sandpaper?

A: **RUFF!**

Q: How do dogs eat spaghetti?

A: With their mouths—
just like everybody else.

Q: What kind of dog
eats with its ears?

A: They all do! Who
removes their ears
before eating?

Q: What do you get when you cross a cocker spaniel, a poodle and a rooster?

Q: **Why did the dog cross the road?**

A: To get to the barking lot!

Q: Why do dogs bury their bones in the ground?

A: Because they can't bury them in trees!

Q: Why do dogs run in circles?

A: Because it's hard to run in squares!

A young girl was visiting her elderly grandfather for the day.

While eating lunch she noticed that the plate looked a bit grimy. 'Are these plates clean, Grandpa?' she asked.

'They're as clean as cold water can get them,' said Grandpa. 'Just go ahead and finish your lunch.'

For dinner, they had hamburgers. The girl thought this plate looked dirty, too. 'Are you sure these plates are clean?' she said.

'I told you,' said Grandpa. 'They're as clean as cold water can get them!'

Later, as the young girl was leaving, her grandfather's dog started to growl and snarl at her.

'Grandpa,' she said, 'your dog won't let me get past.'

'Be quiet, Cold Water!' Grandpa yelled at his dog.

My dog used
to chase people
on a bike.

How did you
stop him?

I took his
bike away.

A dog walks up to the counter in a butcher's. It has a note and cash in its mouth.

The butcher reads the note. It says the dog wants six pork sausages. The butcher takes the money, puts the sausages in a bag and puts the bag in the dog's mouth. The dog leaves. Curious, the butcher follows. The dog goes to a bus stop and sits and waits. When a bus comes, the dog looks at the front of the bus, seems to read where it's going, shakes its head and sits back down. The next bus comes and the dog gets on. The butcher follows. Five stops later, the dog gets off. The butcher follows the dog as it trots up to a house and rams the door with its head once, twice, three times.

The dog's owner opens the door and says, 'So there you are, you dumb dog!'

The butcher says, 'Dumb? That's got to be the most brilliant dog in the world!'

'Brilliant?' the dog's owner says. 'This is the third time he's forgotten his keys!'

Idiot!

Q: When are vets the busiest?

A: When it's been raining cats and dogs.

Q: What did one flea say to the other flea?

A: 'Should we walk or take a dog?'

Q: What type of market should you *never* take your dog to?

A: A flea market!

CLASSROOM CAPERS

Hi, I'm one of the animals at Jill's early learning centre for animals. We learn reading, writing, arithmetic and ROFL-ing ... well, what are you waiting for? Come and join us!

STUDENT: Teacher, would you punish me for something I didn't do?

TEACHER: Of course not. Why?

STUDENT: Well, I didn't do my homework.

A man dug a tunnel out of jail and
came upon a preschool playground.
   'I'm free! I'm free!' he yelled.
   'Big deal,' said a little girl. 'I'm four.'

TEACHER: Which is more important, the sun or the moon?

STUDENT: The moon because it gives us light at night when we need it, but the sun gives us light in the day when we don't need it!

LIBRARY

A boy in a library walks up to the librarian and says, 'I'll have a cheeseburger and chips, please.'

The librarian says, 'You do know you're in a library, right?'

The boy says, 'Oh, sorry,' then he whispers, 'I'll have a cheeseburger and chips, please.'

Q: Why did the pelican get kicked out of the library?

A: Because it had a big mouth.

What are you
reading, Terry?

I don't know.

But you're
reading aloud!

I know, but I'm
not listening.

There was once an inflatable boy, who went to an inflatable school.

All the buildings were inflatable, the teachers were inflatable, even the other students were inflatable. One day the boy got in trouble for bringing a pin to school and was called into the principal's office. The principal glared at him and said, 'You've let me down, you've let yourself down, you've let the whole school down.'

THE FUNNIEST DAY EVER

POP!

There are three types of people in the world—those who can count and those who can't.

TEACHER: What's the name of
the most dangerous city?

STUDENT: Electricity.

DEEP THOUGHTS

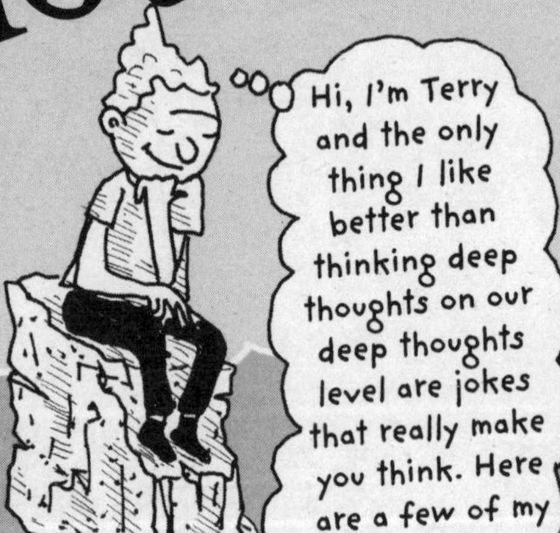

Terry, where are you?

Q: What is nothing?

A: A balloon with the skin scraped off.

I don't know!

Q: What kind of button won't unbutton?

A: A bellybutton.

Q: What is dust?

A: Mud with the juice squeezed out.

Q: How do you make a sausage roll?

A: Put it on a hill and give it a little push.

Q: If you had one arm tied behind your back, how long would it take you to pick the bones out of a sausage?

A: No time at all—there are no bones in a sausage.

Q: What hand should you stir your tea or coffee with—the left or the right?

A: Neither. You stir it with a spoon.

Q: Which word is always spelled incorrectly?

A: Incorrectly.

If you threw a blue stone into the Red Sea, what would it become?

Purple?

Nope. Wet!

Q: What time is it when a dinosaur sits on your fence?

SMASH!

A: Time to get a new fence.

Q: If it took 6 people 6 hours to dig a hole. how long would it take 4 people to dig it?

A: No time at all, because the 6 people have already dug it.

Q: What do you call a
snowman with a suntan?

A: A puddle.

Q: How long should a horse's legs be?

A: Long enough to reach the ground.

Q: What did one ghost say to the other ghost?

A: 'Do you believe in people?'

Q: Three people who were not wearing
hats fell out of a boat into the water,
yet only two got their hair wet. Why?

A: One of them was bald.

A person with a red swollen nose went to see the doctor.

'What happened?' the doctor asked.

'I sniffed a brose,' the patient replied.

'What?' said the doctor. 'There's no "b" in rose!'

The patient replied, 'There was in this one!'

Q: Why did the rabbit go to the hospital?

A: Because it needed a hoperation.

Q: What does a dentist give
a lion with a sore tooth?

A: Anything it wants.

Q: Two mice were out walking. One of them fell into the river. What did the other one do?

A: Performed mouse-to-mouse resuscitation.

A boy went to see a doctor, saying that his body hurt wherever he touched it.

'Show me,' said the doctor.

The boy touched his left shoulder with his finger and groaned in pain. He touched his right shoulder and groaned. He touched his knee and groaned. He touched his ankle and groaned. Everywhere he touched with his finger made him groan.

'I think I know what the problem is,' said the doctor. 'Your finger is broken.'

PATIENT: Doctor, will I be
able to play the piano
after the operation?

DOCTOR: Of course you will.

PATIENT: That's amazing!
Up till now I couldn't!

The patient said to the doctor, 'I feel terrible. I think it was those oysters I ate.'

'Were they fresh?' said the doctor.

'I'm not sure,' said the patient.

'Well,' said the doctor, 'how did they look when you opened the shells?'

'*Opened* the shells?' said the patient.

PATIENT: I feel very weak and I'm extremely hungry.

DOCTOR: Hmm, I see you have a lamington in your ear and a sausage up your nose. Clearly, you're not eating properly.

DOCTOR: What seems to be the matter?

PATIENT: I think I'm a chicken.

DOCTOR: How long have you been feeling this way?

PATIENT: Quite some time, ever since I was an egg.

PATIENT: Doctor, I feel like I'm invisible!

DOCTOR: Next, please.

As a doctor is examining a patient, the nurse bursts in and says, 'Doctor, the patient you just treated collapsed on their way out! What should I do?'

The doctor replied, 'Turn them around so it looks like they collapsed coming in.'

First I got tonsillitis, followed by appendicitis and pneumonia. After that I got poliomyelitis and neuritis. Then they gave me hypodermics and inoculations.

Boy, you had a hard time!

I'll say! I thought I'd never pull through that spelling test!

Q: What did the judge say to the dentist?

A: 'Do you swear to pull the tooth, the whole tooth and nothing but the tooth?'

You know, I must have amnesia. I can't remember a thing.

That's terrible. How long have you had it?

Had what?

PATIENT: Doctor, Doctor, you've got
to help me—I think I'm a bridge.

DOCTOR: What's come over you?

PATIENT: So far, two cars, a truck
and a motorbike.

DOCTOR: I think you need glasses.

PATIENT: But I already wear glasses!

DOCTOR: In that case, I need some, too!

PATIENT: Doctor, I keep seeing into the future!

DOCTOR: I see. When did this first start?

PATIENT: Next Thursday afternoon.

Three friends are marooned on a desert island. One day while walking along the beach, they find a magic lamp. They rub and rub and, sure enough, a genie appears and grants them three wishes—one each.

The first one says, 'I wish I could go home,' and they magically disappear.

The second one says, 'I wish I could go home, too,' and they magically disappear.

The third one starts crying.

'What's the matter?' asks the genie.

'I'm lonely,' they say. 'I wish my friends were still here.'

Three friends are at the top of a huge water slide when they notice a genie. The genie says to them, 'Since there are three of you, I will grant you each one wish. When you are going down the slide, simply shout what you want and it will appear at the bottom when you get there.'

So the first one goes down the slide and shouts, 'A billion dollars!' and lands in a pool of money.

The second one goes down the slide and shouts, 'A lifetime supply of chocolate!' and lands in a pool of chocolate.

But the third one is so excited going down the slide that they shout, 'WEEEEEEEEE!'

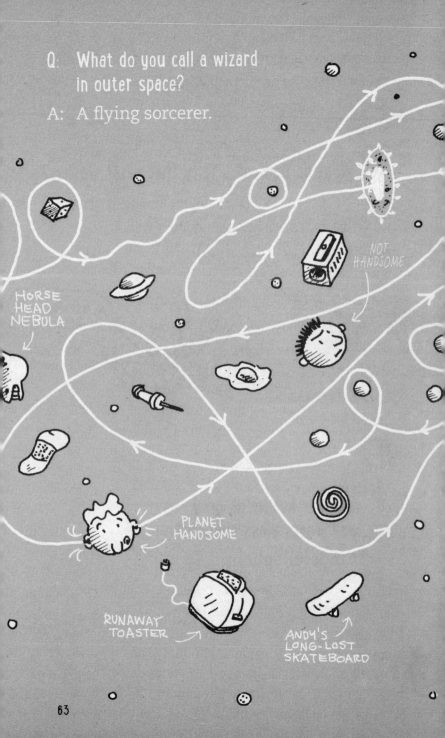

Q: What do you call a wizard in outer space?
A: A flying sorcerer.

NOT HANDSOME

HORSE HEAD NEBULA

PLANET HANDSOME

RUNAWAY TOASTER

ANDY'S LONG-LOST SKATEBOARD

Q: What do you call a fairy that never washes?

A: Stinkerbell.

Q: What is beautiful, grey and wears glass slippers?

A: Cinderellephant!

Q: Who granted the fish a wish?

A: The Fairy Codmother.

Q: What walks through the forest with sixteen legs?

A: Snow White and the Seven Dwarfs.

Q: In the story *Jack and the Beanstalk*, what side of the house did the beanstalk grow on?

A: The outside!

Q: How did Jack know how many beans his cow was worth?

A: He used a cowculator.

Q: What kind of photos do elves take?

A: Elfies!

Q: What is the first thing that witches and wizards do in the morning?

A: They wake up.

Happy Birthday, Terry. I have a poem for you.

Great! Let's hear it.

Don't worry about the past—you can't change it. Don't worry about the future—you can't predict it. And don't worry about the present—I didn't get you one.

What did you get for your birthday?

Older.

Q: Why did the girl get heartburn
after eating her birthday cake?

A: She forgot to remove the candles.

Q: What did the caveman give his wife for her birthday?

A: Ughs and kisses.

Q: Why couldn't cavemen send each other birthday cards?

A: The stamps kept falling off the rocks.

Q: What does every birthday end with?

A: The letter Y.

Knock knock
Who's there?

Abby.
Abby who?

Abby Birthday!

Q: Why are birthdays so good for you?

A: I don't know, but the people who have the most live the longest.

Q: What goes up and never comes down?

A: Your age!

Q: What looks like half a birthday cake?

A: The other half.

Q: What did the cat ask to eat on its birthday?

A: Cake with mice-cream.

Q: What's the hardest thing about being a dragon?

A: Trying to blow out the candles on your birthday cake.

Q: What sort of birthday cake do ghosts like?

A: I-scream cake.

Q: Why did the boy put candles on the toilet?

A: He wanted to have a birthday potty.

HAPPY FAMILIES

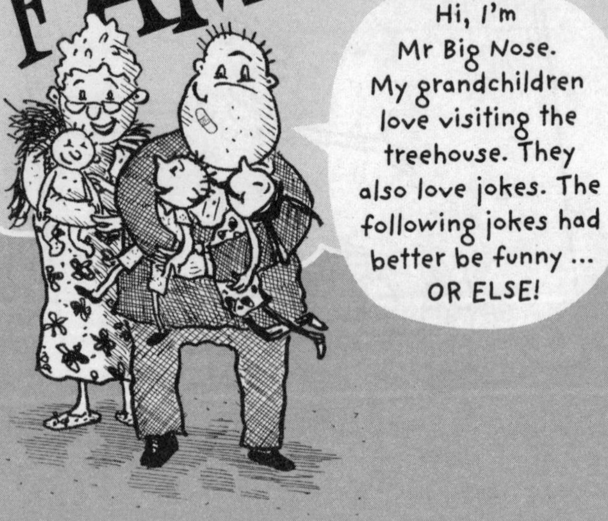

Q: What did the ghost say to its child?

A: Don't spook until you're spooken to.

CHILD: Can I have another glass of water before I go to sleep?

PARENT: Another! But that will be your tenth!

CHILD: I know. My bed's on fire.

CHILD: Mum, I want to go to the zoo.

MOTHER: Listen, if the zoo wants you they can come and get you!

PARENT: How did you do in your history test?

CHILD: Not too well. They kept asking questions about things that happened before I was born.

CHILD: We had a competition at school today to see who could eat the most.

PARENT: Who won second prize?

SON: Cluck, cluck, cluck.

STRANGER: Why is your son clucking?

MOTHER: Because he thinks he's a chicken.

STRANGER: Why don't you tell him he's not a chicken?

MOTHER: Because we really need the eggs.

PARENT: Why did you put a frog
    in your brother's bed?

CHILD: I couldn't find a spider.

Frog and Toad!

'Are bugs good to eat?' the girl asked her father.

'Let's not talk about such things at the dinner table,' her father replied.

After dinner the father said, 'Now, what did you want to ask me?'

'Oh, nothing,' said the girl. 'There was a bug in your soup, but it's gone now.'

A man is washing his car with his son. The son asks, 'Dad, can't you just use a sponge?'

'Oh no,' the kangaroo groaned. 'The weather forecast says it's going to rain.'

'What's the problem with that?' said the rabbit. 'We could use some rain.'

'Sure,' the kangaroo said. 'But it means that my kids will have to play inside all day!'

CHILD: I'm homesick.

PARENT: But this is your home.

CHILD: I know—I'm sick of it.

CHILD: The other kids were
picking on me. They say
I look like a werewolf.

PARENT: Be quiet and
comb your face.

Q: Why do koalas carry their
   babies on their backs?

A: Because it's hard to push
   a pram up a tree.

Q: What's sweet, yellow and extremely dangerous?

A: Shark-infested custard.

Q: Why do sharks live in salt water?
A: Because pepper water makes them sneeze.

Q: What did one shark say to the other shark after eating a clown fish?

A: 'Not only did it look funny, it tasted funny, too.'

Q: What do you call a cow that
   can play a musical instrument?

A: A moo-sician.

Q: What is a pigs favourite game?

A: Snorts and crosses.

Q: **Why did the squirrel cross the road?**

A: Because it had nutting to do.

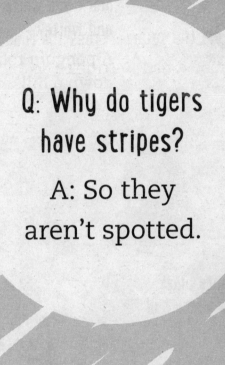

Q: What goes black and white, black and white, black and white, black and white?

A: A penguin rolling down a hill.

Q: What's black and white and laughs a lot?

A: The other penguin that pushed it.

Q: What goes grey, yellow, grey, yellow, grey, yellow, grey?

A: An elephant rolling down a hill with a daisy in its mouth.

Q: What do you get if you cross
a rabbit with an insect?

A: Bugs Bunny.

Q: What did the rabbit say to the carrot?

A: Do you want to grab a bite?

Q: How do you know carrots are good
   for your eyes?

A: Because you never see rabbits
   wearing glasses!

Q: What's a rabbit's favourite dance style?

A: Hip hop.

A man knocks on the door of a house and a woman answers.

'I'm so sorry,' says the man, 'but I accidentally ran over your cat. I'd be happy to replace it if I can.'

'All right,' says the woman. 'But are you any good at catching mice?'

A rabbit walked into a store and asked, 'Do you sell carrots?'

The store owner said, 'No, I don't.'

So the rabbit left.

The next day the rabbit came back again and asked, 'Do you sell carrots?'

The store owner said, 'No, I don't sell carrots!'

The next day the rabbit came back again and asked the store owner if they sold carrots and the store owner said, 'If you ask me if I sell carrots one more time I will superglue your mouth shut.'

The rabbit came back the next day and asked the store owner, 'Do you sell superglue?'

The store owner said, 'No, I don't.'

'That's good,' said the rabbit. 'Do you sell carrots?'

Ha, ha! It's hilarious.

But is it meant to be?

Q: What time does a duck wake up?

A: At the quack of dawn.

Q: Who stole the soap out of the bath?

A: The robber ducky.

Q: What did the duck say when it laid a square egg?

A:

Q: What did the horse say when it fell over?

A: 'I've fallen and I can't giddy-up!'

Two snakes are slithering along in the bush. One turns to the other and asks, 'Are we poisonous?'

'Are you kidding?' says the other snake. 'We're so poisonous that just a single drop of our venom can kill a million rats in seconds! Why do you ask?'

'Because I just bit my tongue ...'

Q: What's the hardest part of milking a snake?

A: Getting the bucket under it.

Q: What's the difference between fleas and elephants?

A: Elephants can have fleas but fleas can't have elephants.

Will you remember my name in an hour?

Sure.

Will you remember my name in a minute?

Yes.

Will you remember my name in a second?

Of course.

Knock knock

Who's there?

You didn't remember my name!

Knock knock
Who's there?

T-rex.
T-rex who?

There is a T-rex at your
door and you want to
know its name?!
Run, you fool!

Knock knock
Who's there?

Dot.
Dot who?

Dot's for me to
know and you
to find out.

Knock knock
Who's there?

Phillipa.
Phillipa who?

Phillipa bath. I need a wash!

Knock knock
Who's there?

Sonja.
Sonja who?

Sonja shoe. I can smell it from here.

Knock knock
Who's there?

Repeat.
Repeat who?

Who. who. who. who ...

PARENT: I see you won a silver medal at camp. What's it for?

CHILD: It's for telling knock knock jokes.

PARENT: And what's that gold medal for?

CHILD: For stopping.

RING!
RING!
RING!

Knock knock
Who's there?

Underwear.
Underwear who?

I underwear my friends are?

Knock knock
Who's there?

Wanda.
Wanda who?

Wanda wish you a happy birthday.

Knock knock
Who's there?

Dishes.
Dishes who?

Dishes me, who are you?

LETTERS & BILLS

Hi, I'm Bill the postman. Delivering the mail is serious business, but that doesn't mean I don't have time for a joke or two ... or three or four ... or five ... or maybe even six. But then I'll have to go. The mail doesn't deliver itself, you know.

Q: What do you get when you
cross a dog with an elephant?

A: A very nervous postman.

Q: What is a postman's favourite herb?

A: Parcel-y.

Q: Why couldn't Jill help Bill
the postman deliver the mail?

A: He wouldn't letter.

Q: What did Bill the postman deliver to Silky?

A: A shopping cat-alogue.

Q: Where do ghosts mail their letters?

A: At the ghost office.

Q: What did Bill the postman
deliver to Dracula?

A: Letters from his FANG club.

Q: How does Dracula start his letters?

A: 'Tomb it may concern.'

Q: What has more letters than the alphabet?

A: The post office.

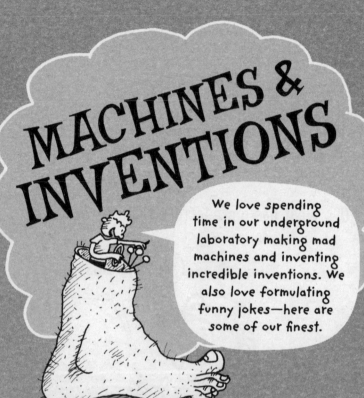

MACHINES & INVENTIONS

We love spending time in our underground laboratory making mad machines and inventing incredible inventions. We also love formulating funny jokes—here are some of our finest.

Q: Why was there thunder and lightning in the lab?

A: The scientists were brainstorming.

A woman brought a very limp parrot into a veterinary hospital. The vet lay the bird on the examination table, pulled out her stethoscope and listened to the bird's chest. The vet shook her head sadly and said, 'I'm so sorry, Polly has passed away.'

Polly's owner said, 'Are you sure? I mean, you haven't done any testing or anything.'

The vet left the room and returned with a large labrador. The dog stood on its hind legs, put its front paws on the examination table and sniffed the dead parrot. The dog then looked at the vet with sad eyes and shook its head.

The vet led the dog out and returned with a cat. The cat sniffed at the bird. Then it meowed, shook its head and walked out of the room.

The vet said, 'I'm sorry. But like I said, your parrot is definitely dead.' Then she went to her computer, hit a few keys and printed out a bill.

Polly's owner took the bill and read it. 'Three hundred dollars!' she cried. 'Three hundred dollars, just to tell me my bird is dead?!'

The vet shrugged. 'If you'd taken my word for it, the bill would only have been fifty dollars, but with the Lab Report and the Cat Scan, what did you expect?'

Q: Where does a scientist wizard work?

A: In a labracadabratory.

Q: Did you hear about the person who fell into an upholstery machine?

A: It's okay, they're fully recovered!

Q: How do scientists freshen their breath?

A: With experi-mints!

Q: What was a more important invention than the first telephone?

A: The second one.

Q: Who was the most famous ant scientist?

A: Albert Antstein.

Q: How do trees get on the internet?

A: They log in.

Q: What do you call a cow with a time machine?

A: Doctor Moo.

Q: What did the scientist say when they saw their time machine?

A: 'Ahh ... this really takes me back.'

Q: What's the best thing about building a time machine for a school project?

A: You can take as long as you want and still get it in by the due date.

A barber claims to have invented a one-size-fits-all hair-cutting machine.

'All you do is put your head in the machine and it does the rest!'

'But that's ridiculous,' says the customer. 'Not everyone has the same size and shaped head!'

'No,' says the barber, 'not at first ...'

SNIP
SNIP

MOVIE MADNESS

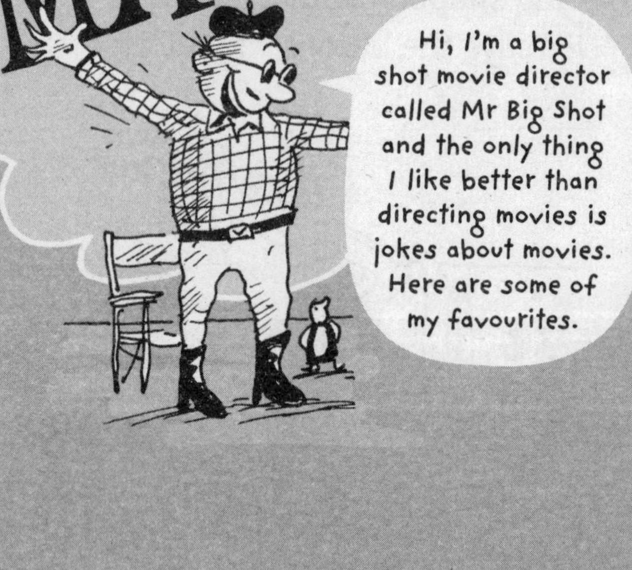

A person was at the movies when they noticed what looked like a toad sitting next to them.

'Are you a toad?' asked the person, surprised.

'Yes,' said the toad.

'What are you doing at the movies?'

The toad replied, 'Well, I liked the book.'

Have you heard of the movie *Constipated*?

No.

That's because it hasn't come out yet.

Q: What do you do if an elephant
    sits in front of you at the movies?

A: You miss most of the movie.

Q: What movie tells the story of
   a pizza maker bitten by a spider?

A: *Spi-dough Man.*

Q: What's an insect's favourite type of movie?

A: Sci-fly.

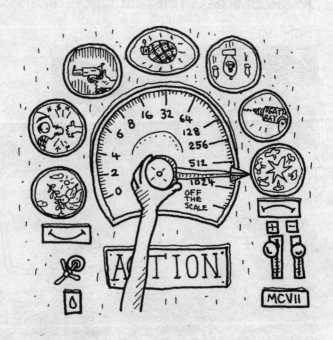

Q: Where does Superman buy his groceries?
A: At the supermarket.

Q: What did Batman say to Robin before they got in the car?

A: 'Robin, get in the car.'

Q: What is a cricketer's least favourite Star Wars movie?

A: *The Umpire Strikes Back.*

NINJAS & SNAILS

Hi, I'm one of Terry's Ninja Snails. When I'm not busy training in the Ninja Snail Training Academy or engaged in top-secret ninja missions, I enjoy cooking, knitting and jokes about ninjas and snails.

A person is at home when they hear a knock at the door. They open the door and see a snail on the porch. They pick up the snail and throw it as far as they can. A few years later there's a knock on the door. The person opens the door and sees the same snail, and the snail says, 'What was that all about?'

One day a snail was robbed by two turtles. When the police arrived and asked what had happened, the snail said, 'I don't know. It all happened so fast!'

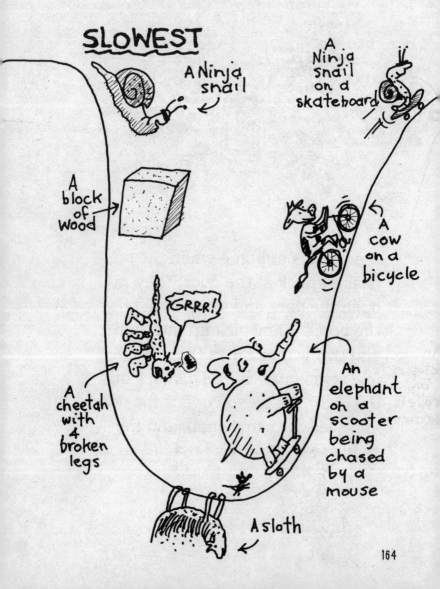

Q: What do you call a snail without a shell?
A: Dead.

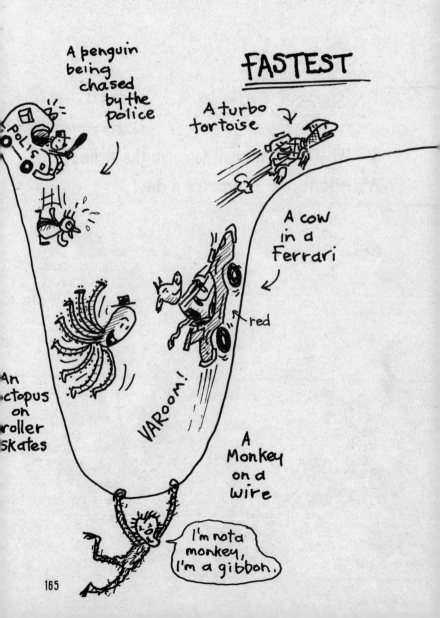

Q: What was the snail doing on the highway?

A: About one kilometre a day!

Very, very slow tortoise.

Ninja Snail

Q: What did the snail say when it hitched a ride on a turtle?

A: 'Wheeeeeeeee!!!!!'

PATIENT: Doctor, Doctor, I think I'm a snail.

DOCTOR: Don't worry, we'll soon have you out of your shell!

Q: What kind of shoes do ninjas wear?

A: Sneakers.

Q: What do ninjas eat at Christmas?

A: Ninjabreadmen.

WHAT SNAILS WOULD LOOK LIKE IF YOU COULD TRAIN THEM TO BE NINJAS.

Q: Why was the ninja so good at baking pastries?

A: Because it had a black belt in martial tarts.

Q: When do you know a snail is lying?

A: When it says it's not home.

Q: What do you call a snail on a ship?
A: A snailor.

PIRATES

Hi, I'm Captain Woodenhead. My pirate crew and I are the most terrifying pirates ever to sail the seven seas, but even terrifying pirates like us love to laugh. Here are some of our favourite pirate jokes.

A pirate and a sailor were exchanging stories. The sailor pointed to the pirate's peg leg and asked, 'How did you get that?'

The pirate said, 'Aye, I wrestled a shark and lost me leg.'

The sailor pointed to the pirate's hook and asked, 'How did you get that?'

The pirate said, 'Aye, I fought Red Beard's crew and lost me hand.'

The sailor pointed to the pirate's eye patch and asked, 'How did you get that?'

The pirate said, 'Aye, a bird came by and left droppings in me eye.'

The sailor said, 'But surely that wouldn't make you lose your eye?'

'Aye,' the pirate answered. 'But it was me first day with the hook.'

Q: **Why do pirates carry swords?**

A: Because swords can't walk.

Q: What did the pirate say when his wooden leg got stuck in the freezer?

A: 'Shiver me timbers!'

Q: What did the pirate say when he turned eighty?

A: Aye—matey!

Q: Why do pirates have so much trouble learning the alphabet?

A: Because they spend so many years at 'C'.

Q: What is a pirate's least
   favourite vegetable?

A: Leeks.

Q: What's a pirate's favourite fish?

A: A goldfish!

Q: What did the pirate do before he buried his treasure?

A: He dug a hole.

Q: When does a pirate buy a ship?

A: When it's on sail.

Q: What kind of snake would you find on a car?

A: A windshield viper.

Two horses were standing at a roadside.

'So, should we cross?' said one.

'No way,' said the other. 'Look at what happened to the zebra!'

Q: What do you call a dinosaur that crashes their car?

A: Tyrannosaurus Wrecks.

PASSENGER: Excuse me, is this my train?

CONDUCTOR: No, it belongs to the railway
company.

PASSENGER: Don't be funny. What I'm
trying to ask is if I can take this train
to Central Station?

CONDUCTOR: No, it's too heavy.

Q: A person who steals is a kleptomaniac. A person who always thinks they are sick is a hypochondriac. But what do you call a person who rides on the top deck of a double-decker bus?

A: A passenger.

POLICE OFFICER: You were doing 120 kilometres an hour in a 60-kilometre zone.

DRIVER: I know! My brakes aren't working and I wanted to get home quickly before I had an accident.

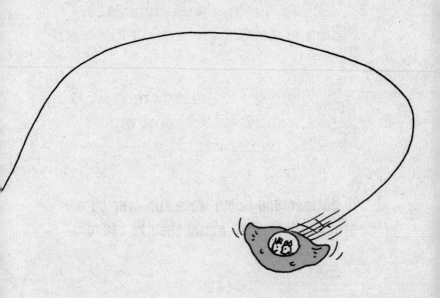

Q: **What is worse than raining cats and dogs?**

A: Hailing taxis.

Q: If Batman and Robin were run over by a
   steamroller, what would they be called?

A: Flatman and Ribbon.

Q: What is green and has four wheels?

A: Grass, I lied about the wheels.

Two toothpicks were walking in a forest when an echidna walked past. One toothpick turned to the other toothpick and said, 'I didn't know that a bus went this way.'

FLIGHT ATTENDANT:
   Would you like dinner?

AIRLINE PASSENGER:
   What are my choices?

FLIGHT ATTENDANT:
   'Yes' or 'no'.

A farm boy accidentally overturned a wagonload of corn on the road.

A farmer who lived nearby went over to have a look and found the boy trying to lift the wagon.

'Hey, Willie,' the farmer said, 'forget your troubles for a spell and come have dinner with us. I'll help you with that wagon afterwards.'

'That's mighty nice of you, but Pa won't like that,' Willie replied.

'Aw, come on, son. Take a break,' the farmer insisted.

'Well, all right then,' the boy finally agreed, 'but Pa won't like it.'

After a hearty meal, Willie thanked the farmer. 'I feel a lot better now, but I know that Pa will be upset.'

'Nonsense,' the farmer said. 'Where is your pa anyway?'

'Under the wagon.'

Q: What do you do if you see a spaceman?
A: Park your car in it, man!

Q: Why did the pelican crash the car?

A: Because pelicans can't drive.

A person applied for a job with an expedition to Antarctica.

'What experience have you had?' asked the expedition leader.

'Well,' said the person, 'I worked on an ice-cream truck for two years.'

A person was driving down the road when they were pulled over by the police. The officer looked in the back of the truck and said, 'Why are these penguins in your truck?'

The driver replied, 'These are my penguins. They belong to me.'

'You need to take them to the zoo,' the officer said.

The next day, the officer saw the same person driving down the road and pulled them over again. The officer saw that the penguins were still in the truck, but they were wearing sunglasses this time. 'I thought I told you to take these penguins to the zoo!'

'I did,' the driver replied. 'And they had such a good time that today I'm taking them to the beach.'

Q: What is white and has long ears, whiskers and sixteen wheels?

A: Two white rabbits on rollerblades!

ANGRY PARENT: How did the car
end up in the living room?

CHILD: Simple. I turned right
at the kitchen.

A cruise ship passes by a remote island, and all the passengers see a bearded man running around and waving his arms wildly.

'Captain,' one passenger asks, 'who is that man over there?'

'I have no idea,' the captain says, 'but he goes nuts every year when we pass him.'

ROBOTS

Hi, I'm Edward Scooperhands the ice-cream serving robot. I'm just one of the many robots who live, work and play in the treehouse. Robots are no joke ... but these robot jokes are.

Q: What did the baby robot call its inventor?

A: Da-ta!

Q: Why did the robot cross the road?

A: Because the chicken was out of order.

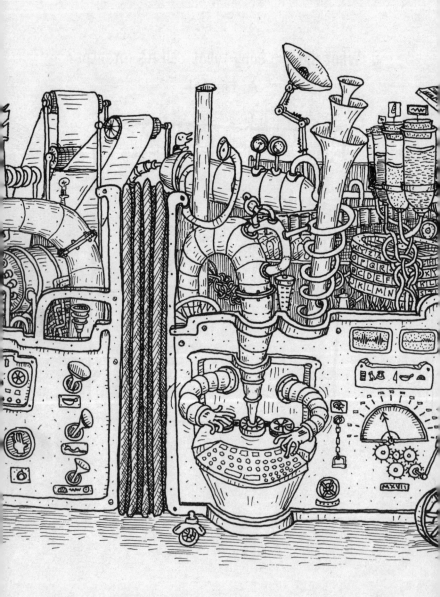

Q: Where do robots sit?

A: On their robottoms.

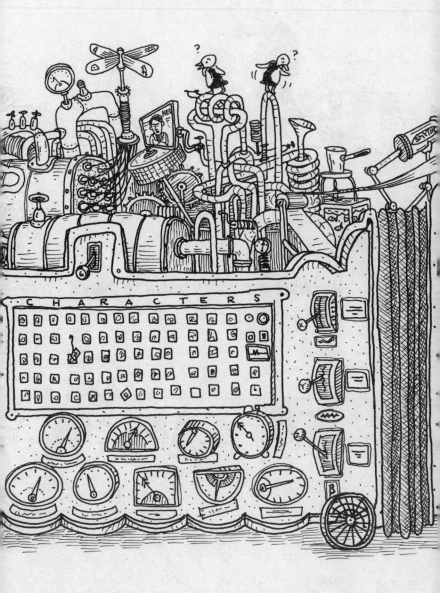

Q: What happens when a robot falls into muddy water?

A: It gets wet and muddy.

Q: What is a robot's favourite snack?

A: Micro chips.

Q: What did the inventor say to their dead robot?

A: RUST IN PEACE.

SILLY JOKES

We're wacky waving inflatable arm-flailing tube men, with lots of jokes to share, like the one about toilet paper and the two about underwear!

Q: Why did the people on the desert island
turn red?

A: Because they were marooned.

Two balloons were in the desert.

One said to the other, 'Watch out for that cactus!'

The other replied, 'What cactussssss ssssssssssssssssssssssssssssss?'

Two inexperienced hunters were hunting in the woods. Before long, they got lost.

'Don't worry,' said the first hunter. 'I heard that if you're lost, you fire three shots in the air so somebody will hear you.'

They fired three shots in the air and waited. A half-hour later they tried it again, and still no one came to help them. Finally, they decided to try it a third time.

'This better work,' said the second hunter. 'These are our last arrows.'

Q. Why did the toilet paper roll down the hill? A: To get to the bottom.

My friends said that onions are the
only food that can make you cry.
So I threw a coconut at them!

Q: What did one
    grain of sand
    say to the other
    grain of sand?

                    A: 'Grittings!'

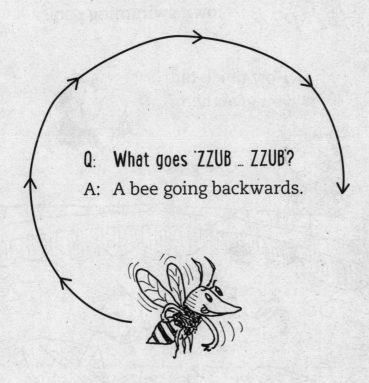

Q: What goes 'ZZUB ... ZZUB'?
A: A bee going backwards.

INNKEEPER: The room is fifty dollars a night, but it's only twenty-five if you make your own bed.

GUEST: Well, in that case, I'll make my own bed.

INNKEEPER: Okay. I'll get you some nails and wood.

Q: What do you call a flower that runs on electricity?

A: A power plant.

Q: What happened when the butcher
backed into the meat grinder?

A: They got a little behind
in their work.

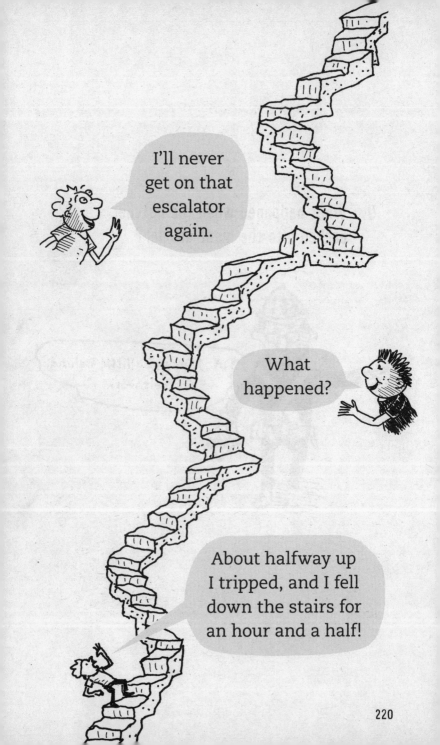

Last night, I had a terrible dream that I ate a giant marshmallow.

Why is that so terrible?

When I woke up, my pillow was missing.

YAWN!

Q: What's Beethoven's favourite food?

A:

Q: What's red and bad for your teeth?

A: A brick.

Q: What kind of music do mummies like?

A: Wrap music.

Q: What goes *Ha-ha, plonk?*

A: A skeleton laughing its head off.

Q: What should you do if your house is surrounded by zombies?

A: Hope like heck that it's Halloween!

Q: What did one snowman say to the other snowman?

A: 'Do you smell carrots?'

Q: What did one volcano
say to the other volcano?

A: 'I lava you.'

Hey, Andy, what are you doing under there?

Under where?

Ha-ha, you said, 'underwear'.

Q: What does a cloud wear under its raincoat?

A: Thunderwear!

I'm not so small.
PLUTO
NEPTUNE
White Hole
URANUS
Thing
Space station
SATURN
Halley's Comet
ings
Laika

Terry, you're eating that banana with the skin on. Why don't you peel it?

There's no need. I know what's inside.

Q: Why did the pelican get kicked out of the restaurant?

A: Because it had a big bill and no money.

DINER: Waiter, Waiter, this egg
is bad. It's old.

WAITER: It is not bad and it's not
old. Eat it up.

DINER: All right, but must I eat
the beak as well?

DINER: Waiter, Waiter, there's a dead fly in my soup!

WAITER: Yes, the hot water killed it.

DINER: Waiter, Waiter, there's a spider in my soup! Get me the manager.

WAITER: He won't come. He's scared of spiders, too.

DINER: Waiter, Waiter, there's a
small slug on my plate!

WAITER: Wait a minute, I'll try and
get you a bigger one.

DINER: Waiter, Waiter, there's
a fly in my soup!

WAITER: Who's there?

DINER: What?!

WAITER: Oops! Sorry, I'm in the
wrong joke!

A bear walked into a restaurant and said, 'I'll have a ham ... ... burger.'

The waiter then asked, 'What's with the big pause?' to which the bear replied, 'I'm a bear.'

Two flies land on a pile of manure. One fly passes gas. The other fly looks at it and says, 'Hey, do you mind? I'm eating here!'

FIRST CANNIBAL: Am I late for dinner?

SECOND CANNIBAL: Yes, everybody's eaten.

DINER: Waiter, Waiter, I'm in a hurry.
Will my pizza be long?

WAITER: No, it will be round.

LOTS OF LAUGHS
AT EVERY LEVEL!

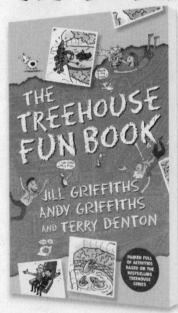

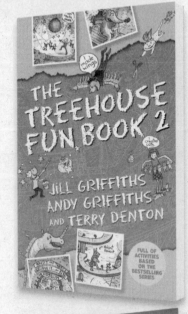

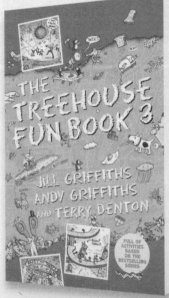

CLIMB HIGHER EVERY TIME